Starting out

Starting this Mood Journal I am feeling...

Colour in the box that shows your mood every day to help keep track

Write a short note about your day - why did you feel like this?

Here's what happened today:

Something that made me happy today:

Something I did just for me:

Stay positive by keeping note of what made you happy each day

Make sure you do something each day just for yourself

Monthly Moods

Colour in everyday to track your mood

D	N	O	S	A	J	J	M	A	M	F	J

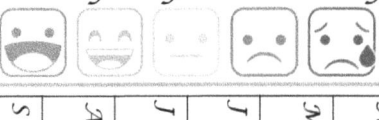

Monthly Tracker

Colour in everyday to track medicine, period or good memories!

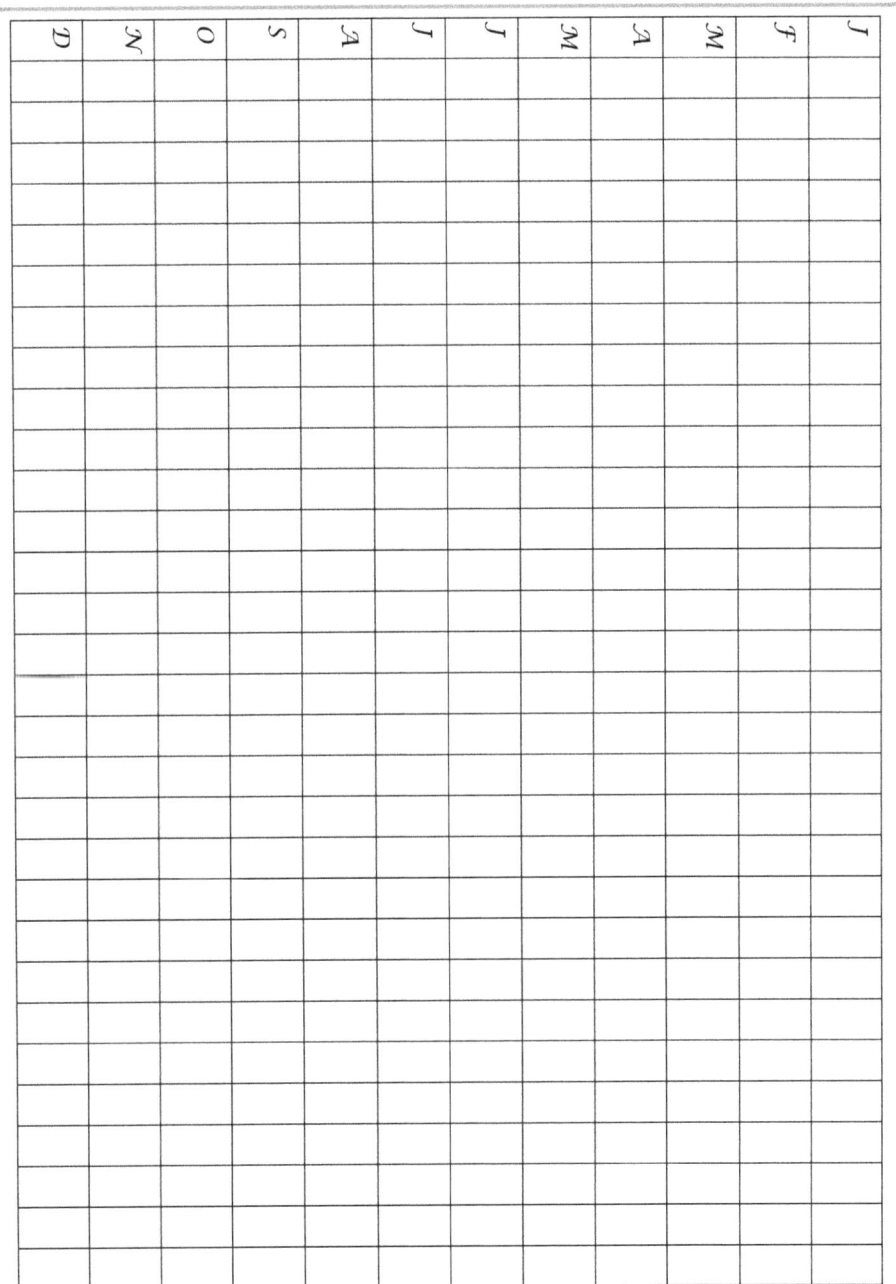

Monday

Let's have a great start to the week!

My Mood Today

Here's what happened today:

Something that made me happy today:

Something I did just for me:

Tuesday

Lets do something nice just for me today!

My Mood Today

Here's what happened today:

Something that made me happy today:

Something I did just for me:

Wednesday

Happy hump day!

My Mood Today

Here's what happened today:

Something that made me happy today:

Something I did just for me:

Thursday

Take time for yourself today!

My Mood Today

Here's what happened today:

Something that made me happy today:

Something I did just for me:

Friday

Push on through to the weekend!

My Mood Today

Here's what happened today:

Something that made me happy today:

Something I did just for me:

Saturday

It's the weekend - let's have fun!

My Mood Today

Here's what happened today:

Something that made me happy today:

Something I did just for me:

Sunday

End of the week! Lets make next week fantastic!

My Mood Today

Here's what happened today:

Something that made me happy today:

Something I did just for me:

My Week

My Mood This Week

Best things that happened this week:

Next week I am looking forward to:

Monday

Let's have a great start to the week!

My Mood Today

Here's what happened today:

Something that made me happy today:

Something I did just for me:

Tuesday

Lets do something nice just for me today!

My Mood Today

Here's what happened today:

Something that made me happy today:

Something I did just for me:

Wednesday

Happy hump day!

My Mood Today

Here's what happened today:

Something that made me happy today:

Something I did just for me:

Thursday

Take time for yourself today!

My Mood Today

Here's what happened today:

Something that made me happy today:

Something I did just for me:

Friday

Push on through to the weekend!

My Mood Today

Here's what happened today:

Something that made me happy today:

Something I did just for me:

Saturday

It's the weekend - let's have fun!

My Mood Today

Here's what happened today:

Something that made me happy today:

Something I did just for me:

Sunday

End of the week! Lets make next week fantastic!

My Mood Today

Here's what happened today:

Something that made me happy today:

Something I did just for me:

My Week

My Mood This Week

Best things that happened this week:

Next week I am looking forward to:

Monday

Let's have a great start to the week!

My Mood Today

Here's what happened today:

Something that made me happy today:

Something I did just for me:

Tuesday

Lets do something nice just for me today!

My Mood Today

Here's what happened today:

Something that made me happy today:

Something I did just for me:

Wednesday

Happy hump day!

My Mood Today
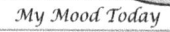

Here's what happened today:

Something that made me happy today:

Something I did just for me:

Thursday
Take time for yourself today!

My Mood Today

Here's what happened today:

Something that made me happy today:

Something I did just for me:

Friday

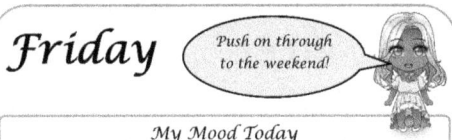

My Mood Today

Here's what happened today:

Something that made me happy today:

Something I did just for me:

Saturday

My Mood Today

Here's what happened today:

Something that made me happy today:

Something I did just for me:

Sunday

My Mood Today

Here's what happened today:

Something that made me happy today:

Something I did just for me:

My Week

My Mood This Week

Best things that happened this week:

Next week I am looking forward to:

Monday

Let's have a great start to the week!

My Mood Today

Here's what happened today:

Something that made me happy today:

Something I did just for me:

Tuesday

Lets do something nice just for me today!

My Mood Today

Here's what happened today:

Something that made me happy today:

Something I did just for me:

Wednesday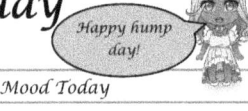

Happy hump day!

My Mood Today

Here's what happened today:

Something that made me happy today:

Something I did just for me:

Thursday

Take time for yourself today!

My Mood Today

Here's what happened today:

Something that made me happy today:

Something I did just for me:

Friday

Push on through to the weekend!

My Mood Today

Here's what happened today:

Something that made me happy today:

Something I did just for me:

Saturday

It's the weekend - let's have fun!

My Mood Today

Here's what happened today:

Something that made me happy today:

Something I did just for me:

Sunday

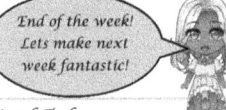
End of the week! Lets make next week fantastic!

My Mood Today

Here's what happened today:

Something that made me happy today:

Something I did just for me:

My Week

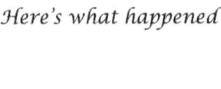

My Mood This Week

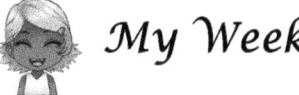

Best things that happened this week:

Next week I am looking forward to:

End of the month!

This month I...

Next month I'm going to make sure I...

Colouring Moods

Monday

Let's have a great start to the week!

My Mood Today

Here's what happened today:

Something that made me happy today:

Something I did just for me:

Tuesday

Lets do something nice just for me today!

My Mood Today

Here's what happened today:

Something that made me happy today:

Something I did just for me:

Wednesday

Happy hump day!

My Mood Today

Here's what happened today:

Something that made me happy today:

Something I did just for me:

Thursday

Take time for yourself today!

My Mood Today

Here's what happened today:

Something that made me happy today:

Something I did just for me:

Friday

Push on through to the weekend!

My Mood Today

Here's what happened today:

Something that made me happy today:

Something I did just for me:

Saturday

It's the weekend - let's have fun!

My Mood Today

Here's what happened today:

Something that made me happy today:

Something I did just for me:

Sunday

End of the week! Lets make next week fantastic!

My Mood Today

Here's what happened today:

Something that made me happy today:

Something I did just for me:

My Week

My Mood This Week

Best things that happened this week:

Next week I am looking forward to:

Monday

Let's have a great start to the week!

My Mood Today

Here's what happened today:

Something that made me happy today:

Something I did just for me:

Tuesday

Lets do something nice just for me today!

My Mood Today

Here's what happened today:

Something that made me happy today:

Something I did just for me:

Wednesday

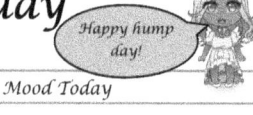

Happy hump day!

My Mood Today

Here's what happened today:

Something that made me happy today:

Something I did just for me:

Thursday

Take time for yourself today!

My Mood Today

Here's what happened today:

Something that made me happy today:

Something I did just for me:

Friday

Push on through to the weekend!

My Mood Today

Here's what happened today:

Something that made me happy today:

Something I did just for me:

Saturday

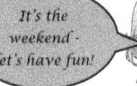
It's the weekend - let's have fun!

My Mood Today

Here's what happened today:

Something that made me happy today:

Something I did just for me:

Sunday

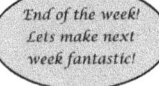
End of the week! Lets make next week fantastic!

My Mood Today

Here's what happened today:

Something that made me happy today:

Something I did just for me:

My Week

My Mood This Week

Best things that happened this week:

Next week I am looking forward to:

Monday

Let's have a great start to the week!

My Mood Today

Here's what happened today:

Something that made me happy today:

Something I did just for me:

Tuesday

Lets do something nice just for me today!

My Mood Today

Here's what happened today:

Something that made me happy today:

Something I did just for me:

Wednesday

Happy hump day!

My Mood Today

Here's what happened today:

Something that made me happy today:

Something I did just for me:

Thursday

Take time for yourself today!

My Mood Today

Here's what happened today:

Something that made me happy today:

Something I did just for me:

Friday

Push on through to the weekend!

My Mood Today

Here's what happened today:

Something that made me happy today:

Something I did just for me:

Saturday

It's the weekend - let's have fun!

My Mood Today

Here's what happened today:

Something that made me happy today:

Something I did just for me:

Sunday

End of the week! Lets make next week fantastic!

My Mood Today

Here's what happened today:

Something that made me happy today:

Something I did just for me:

My Week

My Mood This Week

Best things that happened this week:

Next week I am looking forward to:

Monday

Let's have a great start to the week!

My Mood Today

Here's what happened today:

Something that made me happy today:

Something I did just for me:

Tuesday

Lets do something nice just for me today!

My Mood Today

Here's what happened today:

Something that made me happy today:

Something I did just for me:

Wednesday

Happy hump day!

My Mood Today

Here's what happened today:

Something that made me happy today:

Something I did just for me:

Thursday

Take time for yourself today!

My Mood Today

Here's what happened today:

Something that made me happy today:

Something I did just for me:

Friday

Push on through to the weekend!

My Mood Today

Here's what happened today:

Something that made me happy today:

Something I did just for me:

Saturday

It's the weekend - let's have fun!

My Mood Today

Here's what happened today:

Something that made me happy today:

Something I did just for me:

Sunday

End of the week! Lets make next week fantastic!

My Mood Today

Here's what happened today:

Something that made me happy today:

Something I did just for me:

My Week

My Mood This Week

Best things that happened this week:

Next week I am looking forward to:

End of the month!

This month I...

Next month I'm going to make sure I...

Colouring Moods

Monday

Let's have a great start to the week!

My Mood Today

Here's what happened today:

Something that made me happy today:

Something I did just for me:

Tuesday

Lets do something nice just for me today!

My Mood Today

Here's what happened today:

Something that made me happy today:

Something I did just for me:

Wednesday

Happy hump day!

My Mood Today

Here's what happened today:

Something that made me happy today:

Something I did just for me:

Thursday

Take time for yourself today!

My Mood Today

Here's what happened today:

Something that made me happy today:

Something I did just for me:

Friday

Push on through to the weekend!

My Mood Today

Here's what happened today:

Something that made me happy today:

Something I did just for me:

Saturday

It's the weekend - let's have fun!

My Mood Today

Here's what happened today:

Something that made me happy today:

Something I did just for me:

Sunday

End of the week! Lets make next week fantastic!

My Mood Today

Here's what happened today:

Something that made me happy today:

Something I did just for me:

My Week

My Mood This Week

Best things that happened this week:

Next week I am looking forward to:

Monday

Let's have a great start to the week!

My Mood Today

Here's what happened today:

Something that made me happy today:

Something I did just for me:

Tuesday

Lets do something nice just for me today!

My Mood Today

Here's what happened today:

Something that made me happy today:

Something I did just for me:

Wednesday

Happy hump day!

My Mood Today

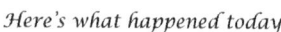

Here's what happened today:

Something that made me happy today:

Something I did just for me:

Thursday

Take time for yourself today!

My Mood Today

Here's what happened today:

Something that made me happy today:

Something I did just for me:

Friday

Push on through to the weekend!

My Mood Today

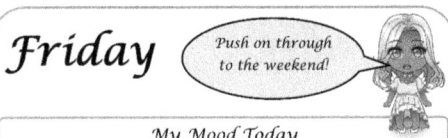

Here's what happened today:

Something that made me happy today:

Something I did just for me:

Saturday

It's the weekend - let's have fun!

My Mood Today

Here's what happened today:

Something that made me happy today:

Something I did just for me:

Sunday

End of the week! Lets make next week fantastic!

My Mood Today

Here's what happened today:

Something that made me happy today:

Something I did just for me:

My Week

My Mood This Week

Best things that happened this week:

Next week I am looking forward to:

Monday

Let's have a great start to the week!

My Mood Today

Here's what happened today:

Something that made me happy today:

Something I did just for me:

Tuesday

Lets do something nice just for me today!

My Mood Today

Here's what happened today:

Something that made me happy today:

Something I did just for me:

Wednesday

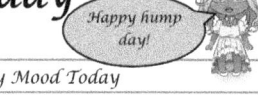
Happy hump day!

My Mood Today

Here's what happened today:

Something that made me happy today:

Something I did just for me:

Thursday

Take time for yourself today!

My Mood Today

Here's what happened today:

Something that made me happy today:

Something I did just for me:

Friday

Push on through to the weekend!

My Mood Today

Here's what happened today:

Something that made me happy today:

Something I did just for me:

Saturday

It's the weekend - let's have fun!

My Mood Today

Here's what happened today:

Something that made me happy today:

Something I did just for me:

Sunday

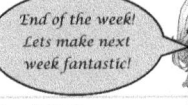
End of the week! Lets make next week fantastic!

My Mood Today

Here's what happened today:

Something that made me happy today:

Something I did just for me:

My Week

My Mood This Week

Best things that happened this week:

Next week I am looking forward to:

Monday

Let's have a great start to the week!

My Mood Today

Here's what happened today:

Something that made me happy today:

Something I did just for me:

Tuesday

Lets do something nice just for me today!

My Mood Today

Here's what happened today:

Something that made me happy today:

Something I did just for me:

Wednesday

Happy hump day!

My Mood Today

Here's what happened today:

Something that made me happy today:

Something I did just for me:

Thursday

Take time for yourself today!

My Mood Today

Here's what happened today:

Something that made me happy today:

Something I did just for me:

Friday

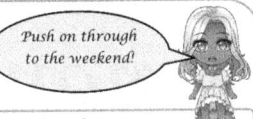

My Mood Today

Here's what happened today:

Something that made me happy today:

Something I did just for me:

Saturday

My Mood Today

Here's what happened today:

Something that made me happy today:

Something I did just for me:

Sunday

My Mood Today

Here's what happened today:

Something that made me happy today:

Something I did just for me:

My Week

My Mood This Week

Best things that happened this week:

Next week I am looking forward to:

End of the month!

This month I...

Next month I'm going to make sure I...

Colouring Moods

Monday

Let's have a great start to the week!

My Mood Today

Here's what happened today:

Something that made me happy today:

Something I did just for me:

Tuesday
Lets do something nice just for me today!

My Mood Today

Here's what happened today:

Something that made me happy today:

Something I did just for me:

Wednesday
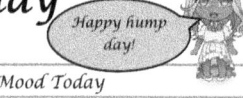
Happy hump day!

My Mood Today

Here's what happened today:

Something that made me happy today:

Something I did just for me:

Thursday
Take time for yourself today!

My Mood Today

Here's what happened today:

Something that made me happy today:

Something I did just for me:

Friday

Push on through to the weekend!

My Mood Today

Here's what happened today:

Something that made me happy today:

Something I did just for me:

Saturday

It's the weekend - let's have fun!

My Mood Today

Here's what happened today:

Something that made me happy today:

Something I did just for me:

Sunday

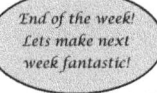
End of the week! Lets make next week fantastic!

My Mood Today

Here's what happened today:

Something that made me happy today:

Something I did just for me:

My Week

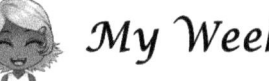

My Mood This Week

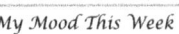

Best things that happened this week:

Next week I am looking forward to:

Monday

Let's have a great start to the week!

My Mood Today

Here's what happened today:

Something that made me happy today:

Something I did just for me:

Tuesday

Lets do something nice just for me today!

My Mood Today

Here's what happened today:

Something that made me happy today:

Something I did just for me:

Wednesday

Happy hump day!

My Mood Today

Here's what happened today:

Something that made me happy today:

Something I did just for me:

Thursday

Take time for yourself today!

My Mood Today

Here's what happened today:

Something that made me happy today:

Something I did just for me:

Friday

My Mood Today

Here's what happened today:

Something that made me happy today:

Something I did just for me:

Saturday

My Mood Today

Here's what happened today:

Something that made me happy today:

Something I did just for me:

Sunday

My Mood Today

Here's what happened today:

Something that made me happy today:

Something I did just for me:

My Week

My Mood This Week

Best things that happened this week:

Next week I am looking forward to:

Monday

Let's have a great start to the week!

My Mood Today

Here's what happened today:

Something that made me happy today:

Something I did just for me:

Tuesday

Let's do something nice just for me today!

My Mood Today

Here's what happened today:

Something that made me happy today:

Something I did just for me:

Wednesday

Happy hump day!

My Mood Today

Here's what happened today:

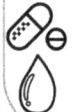

Something that made me happy today:

Something I did just for me:

Thursday

Take time for yourself today!

My Mood Today

Here's what happened today:

Something that made me happy today:

Something I did just for me:

Friday

Push on through to the weekend!

My Mood Today

Here's what happened today:

Something that made me happy today:

Something I did just for me:

Saturday

It's the weekend - let's have fun!

My Mood Today

Here's what happened today:

Something that made me happy today:

Something I did just for me:

Sunday

End of the week! Lets make next week fantastic!

My Mood Today

Here's what happened today:

Something that made me happy today:

Something I did just for me:

My Week

My Mood This Week

Best things that happened this week:

Next week I am looking forward to:

Monday

Let's have a great start to the week!

My Mood Today

Here's what happened today:

Something that made me happy today:

Something I did just for me:

Tuesday

Lets do something nice just for me today!

My Mood Today

Here's what happened today:

Something that made me happy today:

Something I did just for me:

Wednesday

Happy hump day!

My Mood Today

Here's what happened today:

Something that made me happy today:

Something I did just for me:

Thursday

Take time for yourself today!

My Mood Today

Here's what happened today:

Something that made me happy today:

Something I did just for me:

Friday

My Mood Today

Here's what happened today:

Something that made me happy today:

Something I did just for me:

Saturday

My Mood Today

Here's what happened today:

Something that made me happy today:

Something I did just for me:

Sunday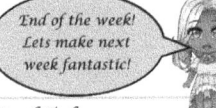

My Mood Today

Here's what happened today:

Something that made me happy today:

Something I did just for me:

My Week

My Mood This Week

Best things that happened this week:

Next week I am looking forward to:

End of the month!

This month I...

Next month I'm going to make sure I...

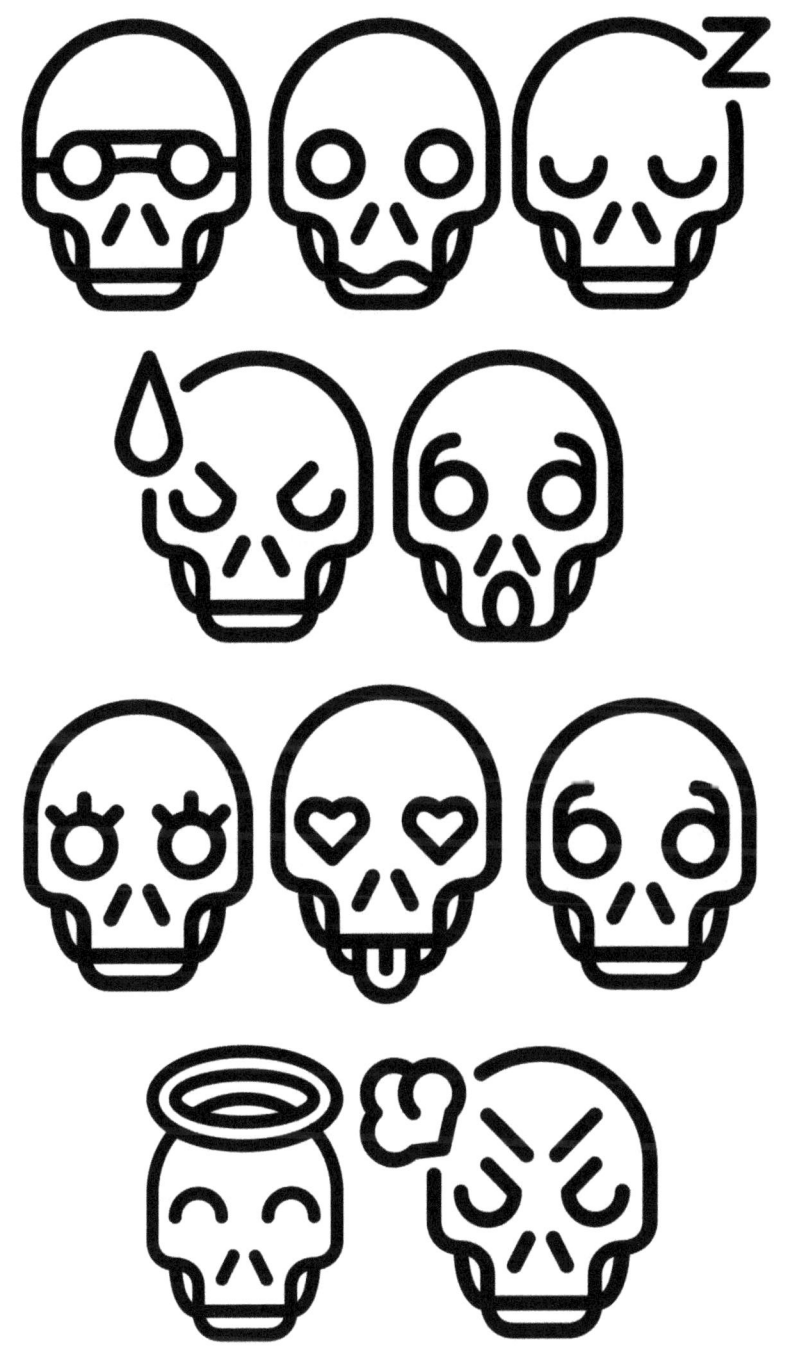

Monday

 *Let's have a great start to the week!*

My Mood Today

Here's what happened today:

Something that made me happy today:

Something I did just for me:

Tuesday

 *Lets do something nice just for me today!*

My Mood Today

Here's what happened today:

Something that made me happy today:

Something I did just for me:

Wednesday

 *Happy hump day!*

My Mood Today

Here's what happened today:

Something that made me happy today:

Something I did just for me:

Thursday

Take time for yourself today!

My Mood Today

Here's what happened today:

Something that made me happy today:

Something I did just for me:

Friday

Push on through to the weekend!

My Mood Today

Here's what happened today:

Something that made me happy today:

Something I did just for me:

Saturday

It's the weekend - let's have fun!

My Mood Today

Here's what happened today:

Something that made me happy today:

Something I did just for me:

Sunday

End of the week! Lets make next week fantastic!

My Mood Today

Here's what happened today:

Something that made me happy today:

Something I did just for me:

My Week

My Mood This Week

Best things that happened this week:

Next week I am looking forward to:

Monday

Let's have a great start to the week!

My Mood Today

Here's what happened today:

Something that made me happy today:

Something I did just for me:

Tuesday

Lets do something nice just for me today!

My Mood Today

Here's what happened today:

Something that made me happy today:

Something I did just for me:

Wednesday

Happy hump day!

My Mood Today

Here's what happened today:

Something that made me happy today:

Something I did just for me:

Thursday

Take time for yourself today!

My Mood Today

Here's what happened today:

Something that made me happy today:

Something I did just for me:

Friday

My Mood Today

Here's what happened today:

Something that made me happy today:

Something I did just for me:

Saturday

My Mood Today

Here's what happened today:

Something that made me happy today:

Something I did just for me:

Sunday

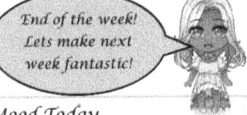

My Mood Today

Here's what happened today:

Something that made me happy today:

Something I did just for me:

My Week

My Mood This Week

Best things that happened this week:

Next week I am looking forward to:

Monday

Let's have a great start to the week!

My Mood Today

Here's what happened today:

Something that made me happy today:

Something I did just for me:

Tuesday

Lets do something nice just for me today!

My Mood Today

Here's what happened today:

Something that made me happy today:

Something I did just for me:

Wednesday

Happy hump day!

My Mood Today

Here's what happened today:

Something that made me happy today:

Something I did just for me:

Thursday

Take time for yourself today!

My Mood Today

Here's what happened today:

Something that made me happy today:

Something I did just for me:

Friday

Push on through to the weekend!

My Mood Today

Here's what happened today:

Something that made me happy today:

Something I did just for me:

Saturday

It's the weekend - let's have fun!

My Mood Today

Here's what happened today:

Something that made me happy today:

Something I did just for me:

Sunday

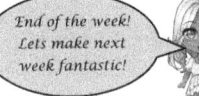

End of the week! Lets make next week fantastic!

My Mood Today

Here's what happened today:

Something that made me happy today:

Something I did just for me:

My Week

My Mood This Week

Best things that happened this week:

Next week I am looking forward to:

Monday

Let's have a great start to the week!

My Mood Today

Here's what happened today:

Something that made me happy today:

Something I did just for me:

Tuesday

Lets do something nice just for me today!

My Mood Today

Here's what happened today:

Something that made me happy today:

Something I did just for me:

Wednesday

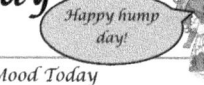
Happy hump day!

My Mood Today

Here's what happened today:

Something that made me happy today:

Something I did just for me:

Thursday

Take time for yourself today!

My Mood Today

Here's what happened today:

Something that made me happy today:

Something I did just for me:

Friday

My Mood Today

😀 😄 😐 🙁 😢

Here's what happened today:

Something that made me happy today:

Something I did just for me:

Saturday

My Mood Today

😀 😄 😐 🙁 😢

Here's what happened today:

Something that made me happy today:

Something I did just for me:

Sunday

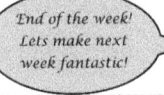

My Mood Today

Here's what happened today:

Something that made me happy today:

Something I did just for me:

My Week

My Mood This Week

Best things that happened this week:

Next week I am looking forward to:

End of the month!

This month I...

Next month I'm going to make sure I...

Colouring Moods

Monday

Let's have a great start to the week!

My Mood Today

Here's what happened today:

Something that made me happy today:

Something I did just for me:

Tuesday

Lets do something nice just for me today!

My Mood Today

Here's what happened today:

Something that made me happy today:

Something I did just for me:

Wednesday

Happy hump day!

My Mood Today

Here's what happened today:

Something that made me happy today:

Something I did just for me:

Thursday

Take time for yourself today!

My Mood Today

Here's what happened today:

Something that made me happy today:

Something I did just for me:

Friday

Push on through to the weekend!

My Mood Today

Here's what happened today:

Something that made me happy today:

Something I did just for me:

Saturday

It's the weekend - let's have fun!

My Mood Today

Here's what happened today:

Something that made me happy today:

Something I did just for me:

Sunday

End of the week! Lets make next week fantastic!

My Mood Today

Here's what happened today:

Something that made me happy today:

Something I did just for me:

My Week

My Mood This Week

Best things that happened this week:

Next week I am looking forward to:

Monday

 *Let's have a great start to the week!*

My Mood Today

Here's what happened today:

Something that made me happy today:

Something I did just for me:

Tuesday

 *Lets do something nice just for me today!*

My Mood Today

Here's what happened today:

Something that made me happy today:

Something I did just for me:

Wednesday

  *Happy hump day!*

My Mood Today

Here's what happened today:

Something that made me happy today:

Something I did just for me:

Thursday

 *Take time for yourself today!*

My Mood Today

Here's what happened today:

Something that made me happy today:

Something I did just for me:

Friday

Push on through to the weekend!

My Mood Today

Here's what happened today:

Something that made me happy today:

Something I did just for me:

Saturday

It's the weekend - let's have fun!

My Mood Today

Here's what happened today:

Something that made me happy today:

Something I did just for me:

Sunday

End of the week! Lets make next week fantastic!

My Mood Today

Here's what happened today:

Something that made me happy today:

Something I did just for me:

My Week

My Mood This Week

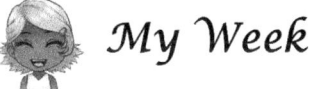

Best things that happened this week:

Next week I am looking forward to:

Monday

Let's have a great start to the week!

My Mood Today

Here's what happened today:

Something that made me happy today:

Something I did just for me:

Tuesday

Lets do something nice just for me today!

My Mood Today

Here's what happened today:

Something that made me happy today:

Something I did just for me:

Wednesday

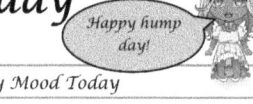

Happy hump day!

My Mood Today

Here's what happened today:

Something that made me happy today:

Something I did just for me:

Thursday

Take time for yourself today!

My Mood Today

Here's what happened today:

Something that made me happy today:

Something I did just for me:

Friday

Push on through to the weekend!

My Mood Today

Here's what happened today:

Something that made me happy today:

Something I did just for me:

Saturday

It's the weekend - let's have fun!

My Mood Today

Here's what happened today:

Something that made me happy today:

Something I did just for me:

Sunday

End of the week! Lets make next week fantastic!

My Mood Today

Here's what happened today:

Something that made me happy today:

Something I did just for me:

My Week

My Mood This Week

Best things that happened this week:

Next week I am looking forward to:

Monday

Let's have a great start to the week!

My Mood Today

Here's what happened today:

Something that made me happy today:

Something I did just for me:

Tuesday

Lets do something nice just for me today!

My Mood Today

Here's what happened today:

Something that made me happy today:

Something I did just for me:

Wednesday

Happy hump day!

My Mood Today

Here's what happened today:

Something that made me happy today:

Something I did just for me:

Thursday

Take time for yourself today!

My Mood Today

Here's what happened today:

Something that made me happy today:

Something I did just for me:

Friday

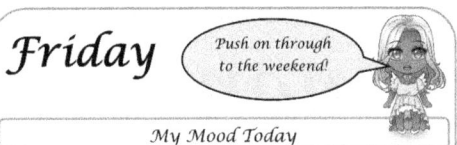

Push on through to the weekend!

My Mood Today

Here's what happened today:

Something that made me happy today:

Something I did just for me:

Saturday

It's the weekend - let's have fun!

My Mood Today

Here's what happened today:

Something that made me happy today:

Something I did just for me:

Sunday

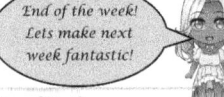

End of the week! Lets make next week fantastic!

My Mood Today

Here's what happened today:

Something that made me happy today:

Something I did just for me:

My Week

My Mood This Week

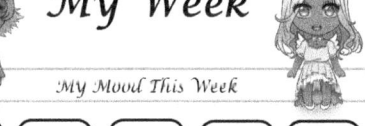

Best things that happened this week:

Next week I am looking forward to:

End of the month!

This month I...

Next month I'm going to make sure I...

Colouring Moods

Colouring Moods

Colouring Moods